THE MARINES

THE
SOCIAL
CORPS

This handbook outlines the Marine Corps' social media principles – to empower Marines to participate with our social media community. The intent is to engage in greater discussion as even better communicators and improved representatives of our Corps.

THE SOCIAL CORPS
marines.dodlive.mil/social-media

COMMANDANT OF THE MARINE CORPS
Gen. James F. Amos

SGT. MAJ. OF THE MARINE CORPS
Sgt. Maj. Micheal Barrett

MARINE CORPS PRODUCTION DIRECTORATE
Greg Reeder, Director (Digital, Social Media and Broadcast)

SOCIAL MEDIA TEAM
Sergeant Mark Fayloga
Sergeant Priscilla Sneden
Sergeant James Shea
Corporal Benjamin Harris

PUBLICATION DESIGN
Bates Creative Group, LLC

MARINE CORPS SOCIAL MEDIA
Marines@dma.mil

MARINE CORPS CYBER SECURITY
HQMC_C4_SNS@usmc.mil

Published in conjunction with the
Marine Corps' Insider Threat Working Group

TABLE OF CONTENTS

FOREWORD

A Message from the Commandant of the Marine Corps

We live in an environment that encourages information sharing and offers ever-increasing opportunities to do so. However, not all information needs to be shared. As Marines, we are aware of our responsibilities to protect classified and sensitive information and do a good job in this area, but we must apply the same vigilance when posting personal information related to Operations Security on social media sites.

The benefits of today's technology include connecting and sharing ideas and information with family and friends in ways we never thought possible just ten years ago. Unfortunately, these same advantages can be exploited by our Nation's adversaries or local criminals who mean us harm. In the course of engaging in social media, we must safeguard against too freely and openly sharing personal information with strangers. Our first line of defense is to understand the threats posed by individuals, organizations, and governments around the world that would use social media and our personal information in nefarious ways.

The Marine Corps Social Media Guide provides critical information that supports our individual and collective efforts to protect ourselves and our families against the potential hazards of information sharing. Read the guide! Understand and apply the information it provides. Make sure your families, friends and fellow Marines understand the importance of protecting personal information. Our Marine Corps and your safety depend on it!

Semper Fidelis,

JAMES F. AMOS
General, U.S. Marine Corps

MARINE CORPS SOCIAL MEDIA PRINCIPLES

Throughout the Marine Corps' history, people have discussed, debated and embraced the United States Marine Corps and our Marines. These discussions continue today through online conversations and social networks. The Corps recognizes the importance of participating in these conversations and has a basic set of social media principles to help empower Marines and our community to participate in the discussion as better communicators and improved representatives of our Corps.

The Marine Corps must continuously innovate to communicate in media-intensive environments, to remain the nation's force in readiness. This mission is based on the Marine Corps Vision and Strategy 2025 and the public affairs tasks outlined in the Marine Corps Service Campaign Plan for 2009-2015.

While building and launching a social media program or accessing a favorite social media site can sometimes be fast, easy, and inexpensive, existing rules for public affairs as well as personal conduct still apply.

The Marine Corps encourages Marines to explore and engage in social media communities at a level they feel comfortable with. The best advice is to approach online communication in the same way we communicate in person — by using sound judgment and common sense, adhering to the Marine Corps' core values of honor, courage and commitment, following established policy, and abiding by the Uniform Code of Military Justice (UCMJ).

The social media principles provided in this handbook are intended to outline how our core values should be demonstrated, to guide Marines through the use of social media whether personally involved or when acting on behalf of the Marine Corps.

 CORE VALUES IN THE SOCIAL MEDIA COMMUNITY

Achieving sustainable credibility online is guided by accepted standards that we live by as American service members. These values should guide participation in the social media process and strengthen organizational credibility.

The Marine Corps strongly adheres to our core values in the online social media community, and we expect the same commitment from all Marine Corps representatives – from Public Affairs and Marine spokespersons to the individual Marine. Deviation from these commitments may be subject to disciplinary review or other appropriate action.

SOCIAL MEDIA FOR LEADERS

While some may assert that social media has improved the way we connect and communicate as a culture, it presents dilemmas for Marine Corps leaders, ranging from being a social media "friend" of a subordinate to "following" those you lead.

The point to consider, though, is that social media is about connecting. Just as Marine Corps leaders may interact and function in their local community alongside their Marines, similar conduct holds true for interacting in the same social media spaces as their subordinates. It is "how" the connections and interactions take place with subordinates that sets the tone for communication. Simply put, online Marine Corps relationships should function in the same manner as any professional relationship would.

With social communication, you essentially provide a permanent record of what you say — if you wouldn't say it in front of a formation, don't say it online. If you come across evidence of a Marine violating command policy or the Uniform Code of Military Justice on social media platforms, you should respond in the same manner you would if you witnessed the infraction in any other environment.

When using social media tools and platforms, everything you say and do as a leader is more visible and taken more seriously. As such, you have a greater responsibility to speak respectfully and intelligently about issues. Remember, when making statements online, you are being viewed as the authority on that topic and may appear to be speaking on behalf of the entire command or even as a spokesperson for the Corps – depending on the audience or venue.

TO FOLLOW OR NOT TO FOLLOW?

 The decision of whether to "follow" or "friend" Marines under their charge on social channels is up to the discretion of individual Marine Corps leaders. Ultimately, it depends on how that leader uses social media. If the leader is using social media as a way to communicate command and unit information, then following members in a leader's command is appropriate. But if the leader is using social media as a way to keep in touch with family and friends, it may not entirely make sense to follow people in their chain of command.

! SELF PROMOTION

Using your rank, job, or responsibilities to promote yourself online, for personal or financial gain, is not appropriate. Such actions can damage the image of the Marine Corps, diminish morale, and reduce unit effectiveness.

PAID SUBMISSIONS

It is against Marine Corps regulations to accept compensation for writing official Marine Corps blogs. Treat requests from nongovernmental blogs for a blog post as a media request and coordinate with your public affairs officer.

ADDITIONAL GUIDANCE FOR LEADERS:

Listen to active audiences to determine how to best engage. The paradigm of telling everyone what they need to know no longer carries significant weight when communicating via social media channels — social media requires, and begins with, listening. If you don't know and understand the audiences you are communicating with, then the interaction will be of limited value. Listening to the online community and complying with Department of Defense policies is paramount to communication success.

You are key to uniting the voice of all Marines using social media speaking on behalf of your command. These Marines must have an accurate understanding of the information that should be communicated to the public in order to ensure accuracy, preserve safety, assure security, and establish credibility.

The Corps' actions are legitimate and, the assumption is, an informed public will agree with this principle. To strengthen this position, the Freedom of Information Act emphasizes the importance of transparency in military activities. We do not "spin" information or stories and do not condone manipulating the social media flow by creating posts designed to mislead followers or control a conversation. Every Web site, "fan page," or other online destination managed by Marines must make that fact known to users.

Marines and staff moderating and managing Marine Corps online presences must be authorized to track and monitor the activity that takes place there. Just as you grant release authority for information by public affairs or unit information Marines, the same authority is applicable for command personnel representing your unit through social media.

Timeliness is defined in terms of the information interests and demands of the public. Empower your Marines to anticipate these interests and effectively balance the timing of communications. The basic guidance for this concept applies: maximum disclosure, minimum delay.

Security of operations, personnel, equipment, information, and facilities must be anticipated and evaluated before information is communicated to the public, such as: preventing the premature disclosure of dates, times and locations of deployments or deployed locations, and homecomings to and from the continental United States or ports of call. For additional details regarding making posts online about the Marine Corps, refer to MARADMIN 365/10 or visit the online resource "Social Media Guidance for Unofficial Posts" at http://www.marines.mil/omg

Privacy of individual service members must be protected. The Privacy Act of 1974 set this principle into law. Marines must remain conscientious with regard to any personally identifiable information that we collect, including how we collect, store, use, or share that information; all which should be done pursuant to applicable privacy policy, laws and information technology rules.

The Marine Corps respects the rights of its Marines to use blogs and other social media tools as a form of self-expression, and also as a means to further explain the Marine Corps' story.

PERSONAL BEHAVIOR – WHAT THE CORPS ASKS OF YOU

Marines are encouraged to responsibly engage in unofficial Internet posting about the Marine Corps and Marine Corps-related topics. The Marine Corps performs a valuable service around the world every day and you are often in the best position to share the Marine Corps story with people we rely on for mission success.

Any content about the Marine Corps or related to the Marine Corps that you personally post on any Internet site is considered an "unofficial internet post." Considerations for what you post includes, but is not limited to, your personal comments, photographs, video, and graphics. The locations where you post the content can be any Internet site, to include social networking sites, blogs, forums, photo and video-sharing sites, and any other online locations (whether or not they are operated or controlled by the Marine Corps or Department of Defense).

ARE YOU UNOFFICIAL OR OFFICIAL?

When you post online content that is not reviewed by any official Marine Corps approval process, you are making an unofficial Internet post. On the flip side, official Internet posts include content that is released by public affairs Marines, Marine Corps Community Services marketing directors, or commander's designated release authorities.

WHAT CAN I SAY ONLINE?

When expressing personal opinions, you must make clear that you are speaking for yourself and not on behalf of the Marine Corps. Plus, making sure the information you post about the Corps is accurate and appropriate isn't enough, you should carefully consider the non-Marine related content you post, since the lines between your personal and professional life are easily crossed when communicating online. Avoid offensive and inappropriate behavior that could bring discredit upon yourself and the Marine Corps. This means that you shouldn't post anything that is defamatory, libelous, obscene, abusive, threatening, racially or ethnically hateful, or otherwise offensive or illegal information or material.

Use your best judgment at all times and keep in mind how the content of your posts will reflect upon you, your unit, and the Marine Corps. Be aware that you lose control over basically everything you post online and that many social media sites like Facebook, Twitter, and YouTube have policies that give them ownership of all content and information posted or stored on their systems. You may have said it, but they own it. What happens online, stays online – and everywhere else.

You are encouraged to professionally and respectfully correct errors and misrepresentations, made by others, about the Marine Corps. However, remember to respond and act with your perspective, not your emotions, when posting content. Refer to your chain of command or public affairs for guidance if you're uncertain about the need for or appropriateness of a response.

If you decide to identify yourself as a Marine, don't disguise, impersonate or otherwise misrepresent your identity or affiliation with the Marine Corps. Stating your rank or grade, billet, military occupational specialty or occupational series, and status (active, reserve, civilian, contractor) is acceptable as well.

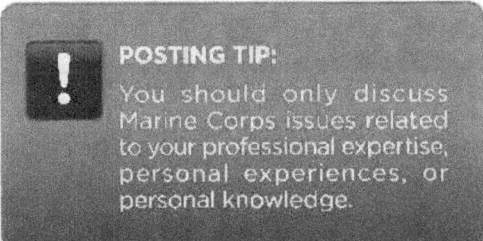

POSTING TIP:
You should only discuss Marine Corps issues related to your professional expertise, personal experiences, or personal knowledge.

Posting or disclosing internal Marine Corps documents or information that the Marine Corps has not officially released to the public is prohibited — period. This policy applies no matter how a Marine comes into possession of a document. Some examples of this information are: memos, e-mails, meeting notes, message traffic, white papers, public affairs guidance, pre-decisional materials, investigatory information, and, most importantly, classified information. You are also prohibited from releasing Marine Corps e-mail addresses, telephone numbers, or fax numbers not already authorized for public release.

Being a Marine, you are no stranger to rules and regulations. This applies to your conduct online as well. When making personal posts or comments, you must continue to comply with regulations and policies related to personal standards of conduct, operations security (OPSEC), information assurance, personally identifiable information (PII), Joint Ethics Regulations, foreign disclosure regulations, and the release of information to the public. Violations of regulations or policies may result in disciplinary action in accordance with the UCMJ. A list of references to polices and regulations are included at the end of this handbook.

THE EAGLE, GLOBE AND ANCHOR

You may use the Eagle, Globe and Anchor; coat of arms (EGA in the center, encircled with words "United States – Marine Corps"); and other symbols in unofficial posts so long as the symbols are used in a manner that does not bring discredit upon the Corps, does not result in personal financial gain, or does not give the impression of official or implied endorsement. You can also contact your local base legal office for an ethics determination, if need be. Marines who violate the Marine Corps' symbols (EGA and/or coat of arms) are potentially subject to legal proceedings. Along these same lines, unless you have permission from the owners, you cannot use any other organization's words, logos or other marks that infringe their trademark, service mark, certification mark, or other intellectual property rights.

The Headquarters Marine Corps, Division of Public Affairs Trademark and Licensing office can give you more clarification about proper use of Marine Corps logos.

IT'S POLITICAL

The Marine Corps encourages Marines to carry out their obligations as citizens – this includes politics. However, there are limitations to your political activity. You can express your political views on public issues or political candidates online, but not as part of an organized communication campaign. If your communication identifies you as a Marine you should clearly state the opinions are yours. You cannot solicit votes for or against a party, candidate or cause. In addition, you cannot participate in any interview or discussion as an advocate for or against a party, candidate or cause. You must adhere to policy in Department of Defense Directive 1344.10 when posting any political content.

It's against federal law for commissioned officers to communicate contemptuous words against the President, Vice President, Secretary of Defense, Deputy Secretary of Defense, Secretary of the Navy, or Governor and Legislature of any state in which he or she is located or performing duty in.

For additional guidance and information on political items of interest, review Department of Defense Directive 1344.10, Political Activities by Members of the Armed Forces. http://www.dtic.mil/whs/directives/corres/pdf/134410p.pdf

BE SAFE OUT THERE!

You should always configure your privacy settings on social networking sites so only people you deem appropriate can view your personal information and photos. Remember, what happens online is available to everyone, everywhere. There is no assumption of privacy for you online. It doesn't end with making sure you understand your basic settings. Online applications you use often have, and share, access to your personal information too: Farmville, Mafia Wars, CityVille, Pandora, SlideShare, DailyMile, Groupon, the Game Center, Foursquare, TweetDeck, TwitPic, the list goes on and on. Although many are good utilities or games, some can load viruses or even use you as an agent to gain access to your friends' and family's accounts.

Recognize a scam when you see one. Getting fooled online happens to thousands of people every day. To avoid being one of those statistics, avoid anything that doesn't initially look legit or just 'shows up' out of context. There are fake sites, inviting posts, passionate comments, and fake fan pages. You might see links or "Likes" of celebrity videos that, when clicked on, claim they are adding something useful to your profile page. There are myriad scams that come in the form of surveys - and the scam creator gets paid if you partake. If it sounds too good to be true, or simply too amazing - it probably is. Scammers know the best way into your profile is playing on your curiosity, emotions, or fears. To stay on top of avoiding the pitfalls of scammers or guarding against them, many social sites provide advice. For example, Facebook has an extensive library of questions and answers regarding third party applications. Searching for "Application security on Facebook" will yield a helpful set of detailed information.

Be extremely careful when disclosing personal details and don't release personally identifiable information such as your social security number, home address or driver's license number. Even providing your birthday and birthplace can give identity thieves or criminals easier access to you and your friends and family. Criminals use the Internet to gain information for unscrupulous activities. By piecing together information you provide on different websites, they can use that information to impersonate you, steal your passwords, steal your identity, and bring harm to you, your fellow Marines or family members. It's your identity – protect it.

You should also guard against cyber criminals and attackers by following sound security procedures. Do not click links or open attachments unless the source can be trusted. Oftentimes, cyber criminals pretend to be people they are not in order to deceive you into performing actions that launch cyber attacks, download viruses, and install malware and spyware onto computers. Aside from damaging your personal equipment, consider the risk to Marine Corps missions and safety if you are responsible for allowing criminal or enemy access to Marine Corps computers or the Corps' network. If you have any questions regarding online security issues, you can contact HQMC C4 cyber security personnel.

BE SAFE OUT THERE CONTINUED...

Consider carefully who you allow access to your social media profiles and personal information. This means, people you allow to be a "friend" on Facebook or add to your friends list on Foursquare, for example. This can also extend to who's in your network on LinkedIn or who you follow (or follows you) on Twitter. Social network "friends" and "followers" may potentially constitute relationships that could affect the outcome of background investigations and periodic reinvestigations associated with your security clearance. Not everyone you know and meet is a good candidate for an online associate.

The best way to secure your stuff is to lock the door. The same holds true to securing access to your accounts by always using strong passwords. To protect your online and social media accounts from getting hacked you should set a good, strong password that has at least 14 characters comprised of lower and upper-case letters, numbers, and symbols. As an added protective measure you should also frequently change your passwords.

Social media, marketers, businesses – and the bad guys are all interested in where you are. Because of this, you must be aware of using the Global Positioning System and geotagging features of your devices and social accounts. For example, in some situations when you geotag photos and use location-based social networking applications (like Foursquare) the geographical location information you disclose can be devastating to Marine Corps operations. You should avoid tagging photos with geographical location when loading to photo sharing sites like Flickr and Picasa. When you're deployed or in an operational setting or training location, turn off the GPS features of your electronic devices and don't report location in social media or social sharing applications. Failure to do so could result in mission failure, harm to you or other Marines, and can put family and friends at risk.

REMINDERS FOR YOUR ONLINE BEHAVIOR

Remember, there's a big difference between speaking "on behalf of the Marine Corps" and speaking "about" the Marine Corps. For every Marine, pay close attention to the following guidelines.

There are rules

All Marines, from officers to enlisted, must adhere to Department of Defense policy, Secretary of the Navy Instructions, and Marine Corps Orders and Directives related to online media in every public setting. A guide to the most applicable references is provided at the end of this handbook.

You are responsible for your actions.

Anything you post that can potentially tarnish the Marine Corps' image is your responsibility. The Marine Corps encourages you to participate in social media, but urges you to exercise sound judgment and common sense. Don't let a careless mistake or ill thought, comment, or post hamper your career or the Corps' history and traditions.

Let subject matter experts respond to negative posts.

You may come across negative or disparaging posts about the Marine Corps or see others trying to spark negative conversations. Unless you are a trained and official Marine Corps online spokesperson avoid the temptation to react. Refer the posts or links to the conversation to your public affairs office.

Mixing your professional and personal relationships

Online, your personal and professional personas are likely to intersect. While the Marine Corps respects the free speech rights of all Marines, remember that civilians, fellow Marines and leaders often have access to the online content you post. Everything you publish online has the potential to be seen by everyone – not just your friends and family. Content you post or that others post about you can be forwarded as well. A seemingly simple, somewhat private post can, and may, be shared with thousands or more people and is nearly impossible to retract once it has entered the public arena.

NEVER disclose any information that compromises Operations Security (OPSEC) or foreign disclosure policy. NEVER disclose information that is intended for official use only. ALWAYS be aware that taking public positions online that are counter to the Marine Corps' interests could cause, or result in, personal conflict.

Marines should contact their local public affairs office for questions about personal or unit involvement in social media. For answers to social media questions, cyber security concerns, or trademark interests, or to get top-level guidance and support you can take advantage of the following points of contact:

Marine Corps	Marine Corps Trademark	Headquarters Marine Corps
Social Media Office	and Licensing Office	Cyber Security
P 703-602-3013 or 5193	P 703-614-7678	P 703-693-3490
Marines@dma.mil	Trademark_Licensing@usmc.mil	HQMC_C4_SNS@usmc.mil

MARINE CORPS DIGITAL – FLAGSHIP PROPERTIES

	Website	www.marines.mil
	Blog	marines.dodlive.mil
	Magazine	marinesmagazine.dodlive.mil
	Broadcast	www.marines.mil/MarinesTV
	Facebook	facebook.com/marines
	YouTube	www.youtube.com/marines
	Twitter	www.twitter.com/USMC
	Flickr	www.flickr.com/marine_corps
	Social Media Inbox	Marines@dma.mil

Understanding Facebook Tracking and How to Set Privacy

Protect Your Facebook Account

The best way to protect your privacy and prevent Internet related crimes like identity theft on Facebook is by maintaining your privacy settings.

Ways Facebook Can Track You

With the use of the social networking site's social plug-ins, Facebook learns what websites you visit while you're logged into Facebook. Additionally, Facebook, as with other websites that employ the use of "cookies" can also continue to keep a record of your activity even after you are logged out while you are offline.

Social plug-ins, that allow you to see which of your friends have also visited the same website, create what Facebook hopes will be a more socially interactive and personalized experience for their users. Although you may have been informed about this type of data collection up front, you might not have paid attention to the fine print and are unaware you're being tracked.

One third of Facebook's traffic is created by mobile users. With that in mind, Facebook launched a GPS-based application called Facebook "Places" that allows users to virtually "check in" to various locations like restaurants, shops, or other venues via a mobile phone.

Facebook Places is potentially dangerous since any "Friends" can check anyone else into a location – unless the setting is disabled.

To disable the "check-in" setting:

- Log into your Facebook account and click on the drop down arrow located on the upper right hand corner of your screen.

- Drop down on the list and click "Privacy Settings."

- Under the "How Tags Work" section, click "Edit Settings" and then turn off the link that states "Friends Can Check You Into Places." A new pop-up page will appear.

- Choose the drop down selection item for "Disabled" next to the text that states "Friends can check you in using the old mobile places app."

- Click the "Okay" button to apply.

To disable Facebook Places on your mobile device to prevent people from checking into your personal locations, navigate to the options setting on your cell phone and uncheck "Share my location with Facebook."

Controlling Privacy While Using Apps, games and websites

By way of apps, games and web surfing, third parties can access information about Facebook users. In the past, these third parties had the ability to collect any information that users granted them access to in their profiles. More recently, however, Facebook has added a feature in which third-party developers can also access users' contact information (including current addresses and mobile phone numbers), a power not previously granted. Facebook users may unknowingly opt-in to this feature when they allow apps to access their information via the Request for Permission window.

To protect your privacy while using apps, games and other websites, follow these steps:

1. Log into your Facebook account and click on the drop down arrow located on the upper right hand corner of your screen.

2. Click "Account Settings."

3. Select the "Apps" item from the left hand column on the page. The "App Settings" page should be shown on the right. By default, applications on Facebook have access to your friends list and any other information you have chosen to share with everyone. On this page, you'll want to make some significant changes.

4. The page shows all the apps you have authorized to interact with your Facebook account. Click the "x" on the right side of your screen to delete any unwanted apps that you may no longer use. Click "Remove" on the popup window that appears to apply. If a second pop-up window appears to confirm, click "Okay." Continue this step for all other apps that you want to delete. *Tip: Facebook does not actually guarantee that information you've already shared with a third party will be deleted. Instead, they recommend that users contact the application developers directly.*

5. For the apps you want to keep and to choose who can see your app posts and activity click the "Edit" link next to each app. A list of profile information that the app has access to appears. You will notice that most apps have access to a tremendous amount of your information. If you are uncomfortable with these settings, click "Remove app" at the top of this list, click "Remove" on the pop-up window, and then click "Okay" to confirm. Otherwise, look for the label "App activity privacy."

6. Next to the activity privacy label choose the drop down list and select the level of privacy you want. The most restrictive default level is "Friends except acquaintances" the least is "public" which shares your app activity with anyone on Facebook. If you want to remove all app activity view options, choose the "custom" list item then select "Only Me" from the list of people to make the app visible to.

7. Once you've completed all the app settings, click "Close" to return to the full app list. Continue this step for all other apps that you want to examine.

8. After completing the account settings for apps, navigate to your privacy settings and select the link for "Apps and Websites" and click on "Edit Settings."

9. From here, there are more options to control your privacy, the first of which is "How people bring your info to apps they use." Click on the "Edit Settings" button.

10. On the resulting pop up window you can determine what information of yours your friends can also share. This means that if you share something on Facebook, anyone who can see it can share it with others, including the games, applications, and websites they use. You can find out more detailed information on the categories of shareable information at http://www. facebook.com/about/privacy/your-info-on-other#friendsapps

11. After making your category choices, click on "Save Changes" then "Okay."

12. Last but not least, under the "Public search" section, click "Edit settings" on the right side of your screen. A new page will open. Uncheck "Enable public search" to keep your profile out of Facebook's search engine.

13. Click "Back to apps" to return to the previous page.

Changing the past

If you have ever shared something with all your friends, then later wished you could limit who could see it, Facebook also provides an option to change the audience for something after

you post it, much the same way as the settings occur as with apps outlined above.

To enable this feature, navigate to your privacy settings and choose the option to "Limit the Audience for Past Posts" by clicking on the link labeled "Manage Past Post Visibility." This will turn the option on for all your previous posts and allow you to custom select the type of audience (Friends, Friends except acquaintances, etc.) for each.

Reviewing your photo tags

From the "How Tags Work" section within your privacy settings you can turn on (or off) the "Tag Review" option. Turning this option on allows you to review tags friends add to your content before the tags appear on Facebook. Plus, when someone who you're not friends with adds a tag to one of your posts you'll always be asked to review it. When you approve a tag, the person that is tagged and their friends can see your post.

Remember: It's important to check your privacy settings for apps, games and websites fairly often, as you may grant access to your information to new applications without even realizing it. There is also the potential for Facebook to change your settings back to the default for privacy or security when they add new security features.

Some excerpts provided by 2011 Guide to Facebook Privacy, http:// www.myid.com

YOU'RE THE SOCIAL MEDIA MARINE – NOW WHAT?

If you hold a public affairs occupational specialty or are assigned to official unit information duties, you are usually the "go-to expert" when it comes to social media. Personnel assigned to Marine Corps Community Service organizations play an important role in social media production as well. Regardless of how you were chosen, what your background is, or even how much you know about the field of social media, everyone who represents the Corps in social communications has a unique opportunity to provide an inside perspective to the Marine Corps' reputation online and to engage in potentially thousands of online conversations about the Marine Corps every day. It truly is a great opportunity and puts you at the forefront of telling the Corps' interesting story.

With the assignment to managing and conducting social media on behalf of the Marine Corps, you must remember: everything you do balances on public trust – this is the foundation upon which the success of public affairs and social media is built. Trust must be given freely, it cannot be mandated.

As part of your duties, you will actively engage the public, ensuring that you consider and promote unity of voice, freedom of information, timeliness, and accuracy while maintaining security, and privacy.

PROFESSIONAL BEHAVIOR - GUIDANCE FOR OFFICIAL POSTS

Marine Corps units and organizations, Commanders, Public Affairs Marines, subject matter experts, and individual Marines engaging social media should use their best judgment when posting and responding to topics on social media sites. To help outline that judgment, keep in mind some basic pointers when interacting online:

- **You *are* the Marine Corps.** As a Marine, it is important that official posts convey the same journalistic excellence the Marine Corps instills in all of its communicators and public affairs professionals. Be respectful of all individuals, races, religions and cultures; your conduct is a direct reflection on the Marine Corps. When you are communicating on behalf of the Corps to the recipient, you embody what the Marine Corps is all about.

- **Get approved.** Have a method in place to ensure there is a thorough content review before posting – conduct a security review, being mindful of OPSEC and foreign disclosure directives, for official use only information, and content subject to the Freedom Of Information Act. All your posts and comments should still follow the basic guidelines for information release: all content protects security, is accurate, is proper, and complies with all applicable policy. Nobody is perfect - making sure the content workflow or review process is in place up front reduces the chance of errors or faulty posts down the road.

- **Provide meaningful content.** If your complete thought, along with its context, cannot be squeezed into a character-restricted space (such as Twitter), then provide a link to an online location where you can express it completely and accurately. If you loose the reader through confusing communication, you'll never be able to explain a thought or concept about the Marine Corps or the Corps' position on a topic.

- **Respond to all *necessary* topics and comments.** This is an opportunity to leverage social tools for what they are - a means of communication. Avoid the tendency to defend and protect every comment made, though. Given time, social networks normally self-correct negative comments, posts or misinformation. If an official position or expert opinion is required - that's your cue to join in. Replace errors or misrepresentations of the Corps with fact, not argument.

- **What happens online... is permanent.** This may be nice if leaving your memoirs for posterity, but it is more ominous than that -- anything you write online will never disappear. Take great care in what you do or say online. Aside from being published, and essentially part of a permanent record -- even if you "remove" or "delete" it later or attempt to make it anonymous, the information is released and distributed at high velocity. Information, pictures or details you post, a reposting of your comments, or information about the Marine Corps posted by others is also permanent and most likely forever beyond your control to remove.

- **Negative comments will happen.** An open forum comes with certain risk of negativity and to shy from it may tarnish your credibility. Don't join in with an emotional or passionate rant or response, though. What you say and how you respond should be reviewed and approved to ensure you accurately express the Corps' position without editorializing or straying from the facts.

- **Allow your fans to fight for what they believe in.** Fans are not the official Corps' responders. However, they carry with them a different level of credibility and garner trust from the community in their own right. Let them respond, vent, praise, pontificate, comment and discuss. This is what social media does best – it connects people and ideas.

- **Give fans and followers consideration.** You should only delete or block comments, or ban users when there is a clear pattern of malicious, derogatory behavior or when those users are in violation of the terms of participation and use of your site. Hate speech, online attacks, bullying, and inappropriate behavior should be spelled out in your terms of use. Most social users understand the rules of the road. Generally speaking, the fan base is looking to you to make sure everyone behaves. If they aren't breaking the rules, let them communicate.

- **Stay in your lane.** Do not comment on what you do not know. Always gather the facts, know the rules, understand the audience, and be familiar with the medium through which you are communicating.

- **Keep records.** If you manage a Marine Corps social media presence, then you need to keep records of your online interactions and conversations. Official Marine Corps statements may be held to the same legal standards as traditional media communications. The types of records to keep include any direct, online dialogue FROM the Marine Corps. You don't need to capture all the inbound or user generated content, but you should be keeping track of what you say and produce. Your Twitter feed, Facebook posts, replies to comments, blog posts, and responses to queries are all examples of communications to keep on file.

- **Don't violate others.** DO NOT claim to have authored something that is not yours. If you are using or referring to someone else's content, credit them for it in your post and ask them if you can use their content. Do not use copyrights, trademarks, publicity rights, or other rights of others without the necessary permissions from the owners.

- **Don't overdo it.** Closely monitor all your discussion threads or comment responses but don't over moderate.

- **Play by the rules.** Follow all applicable Department of Defense, Secretary of the Navy, and Marine Corps rules and regulations with regard to social media, OPSEC, PII, information release, information assurance, foreign disclosure, internet use, ethics, freedom of information, politics and public affairs.

WHAT TO CONSIDER BEFORE YOU BECOME
A SOCIAL MEDIA SITE OWNER

How are you going to pull this off?

Identify who will be your social media managers, who will post, who will moderate, who will manage the community, what metrics to track, how often and when to post, the types of content you plan to share, etc. Make sure you have contingency plans in place to allow for others to cover established duties. There are myriad resources online that offer advice on this topic. A lot can be done with very few staff – as long as you plan adequately.

Why are you doing this?

What do you want to achieve? What do you plan to communicate? Are you planning on distributing command information, connecting to a community, building esprit de corps? The list will depend on your circumstances but you should define the goals up front so you have a road map to follow – or at least start with.

Who are you talking with?

Identify the audience you intend to communicate with. This can include Marines, Marine Corps families, Veterans, civilians, and the general public. Don't forget, your audience will still touch those you may not have specifically planned on such as your stakeholders, elected officials, community leaders, and adversaries or enemies.

You have to review the policy – really.

Before you get started with social media, it's important to understand Marine Corps social media policy. Marine Corps social media resources can be found at: http://www.marines.mil/socialmedia.

Pick and choose where to post, wisely.

Identify the social media platforms that will be best suited for the needs of your organization. Not all platforms will work for some, so make sure you understand what can be achieved with each. Look at what other organizations are doing to get ideas. You don't necessarily have to be on Facebook AND Twitter AND YouTube. Where you decide to communicate is a function of whom you're talking with and how many you have to accomplish your plan.

Draft your content strategy.

After identifying your audiences and selecting the platforms, draft a posting strategy. This helps refine your organization's social media goals.

Develop your own rules and training.

You and your team will be responsible for developing organization-specific social media policies or procedures, such as additional posting and commenting policies. Also make sure to develop training materials to help educate and train individuals in your command about social media, online protection, and the proper use of the social space.

UNIT SOCIAL MEDIA SITE REGISTRATION

If you are managing an official Marine Corps social media site, you must register the site in the Corps' central directory. The site registration page can be found at the Corps' Social Media page (http://www. Marines.mil/socialmedia).

From a rules and regulations perspective, official unit social sites must comply with Marine Corps public affairs policy or guidelines. Commands are also ultimately responsible for content posted on their platforms. Develop a good set of operating guidelines, disclaimers and terms of use to help guide your actions and those of your fans. See the section below "Set up ground rules for your fans..." for more info.

Aside from the rules, though, there are benefits of listing your site in the directory:

Once your site is reviewed and approved, it will be listed in both the Corps' and Department of Defense official social media directories.

Your unit / Command Fan site will be submitted to Facebook to have ads removed (corporate endorsement is prohibited on our official pages).

Your site registration gives the site owners (Commander) limited legal protection through U.S. Government or Department of Defense Terms of Service agreements.

Registered, top-level Marine Corps unit, base, or station social media sites may be eligible for inclusion in Corps wide social media management platforms.

MARINE CORPS SOCIAL MEDIA SITE REGISTRATION:
http://www.Marines.mil/socialmedia/.

Step-by-step instructions for Terms of Service agreements for Facebook and YouTube can be found at the following links:
YouTube: https://forum.webcontent.gov/?page=TOS_YouTube
Facebook: https://forum.webcontent.gov/?TOS_Facebook

EIGHT STEPS TO SETTING UP YOUR OFFICIAL SOCIAL MEDIA SITE:

1. Approval from you Commanding Officer or Public Affairs Officer. The release authority must approve an official social media site before it can be registered.

2. Be an authentic military source. The point of contact setting up and registering the site must have a valid ".mil" email address when submitting for approval.

3. Your social media site must relate to an official Marine Corps website. Social media communications are based on an official military reference. This should be your command's website, your higher headquarters site, or Marines.mil if your organization does not have a website.

4. Posted disclaimers. The disclaimer identifies the page as an official Marine Corps social media presence and disclaims any endorsement. This keeps everything above board for your community, you, and your social media host.

Sample Disclaimer: *This is an official Marine Corps page. However, the appearance of hyperlinks does not constitute endorsement by the U.S. Marine Corps. The U.S. Marine Corps does not exercise any editorial control over the information you may find at linked locations.*

5. Identify your site as "official." One of the keys to social media is transparency – to build trust and let your fans know with whom they are dealing. If you're a site that represents recruiting efforts, for example, identify the site as such. You also need to let the fans know that the site is official, so they understand that what you post there is done with an assumption of authority. A convenient place for one of the official markings is on the left hand info icon (tab) in Facebook or directly in your profile description on Twitter.

6. Official sites should be open to the public. "Private" Facebook groups won't be considered for listing on the Marine Corps's social media directory.

7. Sites should be labeled on Facebook as "Organization-Government." The use of any category or type other than a Government Fan page violates the government's terms of service agreement with Facebook. Make sure YouTube channels are set up as a government presence as well.

8. Set the default view of your Facebook wall to show only posts from your organization. Setting the default to show only your posts does not limit fan activity, rather it helps guide the conversation. Fans can still see their Friends activity or all posts on the fan site by choosing the related links for those items from the Facebook wall.

SOCIAL MEDIA MEASUREMENT AND METRICS

Social media measurement is about more than just numbers. It's about trends and human feedback. Sites like Facebook, Twitter, Flickr, and YouTube allow for administrators to track views, impressions, and comments. Many social sites provide their own analytics as well. And, there are third party vendors that offer metrics and social media monitoring tools.

By using all the data these various options offer, in conjunction with comments and reader feedback, it's easier to determine how organizational messages are received and how the community is responding to the content. Using the analytics tools of each platform can help a unit demonstrate the usefulness of a social media platform, and even highlight the success of a specific social media campaign.

There are a few Corps wide agreements, and other military services using various monitoring applications that you may be eligible to use or integrate with. To find out more, visit the Marine Corps' Social Media page (http://www.marines.mil/socialmedia) or contact the Marine Corps Production Directorate, Social Media team for more details (marines@afn.dma.mil).

Facebook Insights: measurements of details that give Facebook site owners and administrators the ability to understand and analyze trends for their user growth and demographics, consumption of content, community involvement, and creation of content so they are better equipped to improve and manage the online community.

Feedback percentage: a measurement of Facebook comments and likes, computed as: (comments + likes)/Impressions. It does not account for other user actions such as video plays and link clicks. This is one method of determining what types of posts and content Facebook fans find useful.

Facebook Interactions: a collection of specific trends available on Facebook Insights that includes measurement of your comments, wall posts, and likes. The totals provided through interactions helps you to understand how effective your posts and content are, in engaging your audience.

YouTube: Channel views and Upload views: Chanel views represent the volume of visits to a specific YouTube channel page (i.e. http://YouTube.com/Marines). Upload views is the actual total number of views for all uploaded videos by a user or account. For example, the Marines channel video "Making Marines - A Drill Instructor Story" has more than 200,000 upload views.)

Unique page view: commonly tracked statistic to log the number of different visitors a website receives in a given time period.

SET UP GROUND RULES FOR YOUR FANS – AND FOR YOU

If you are going to hold fans accountable for their actions, you need to spell out what your expectations are and how you intend to interact as well. A good way to do this is posting a policy statement on any social networking sites where you host content. To be considered an official Marine Corps social media site, you must post the following terms of use on each social media site you establish.

Terms of use for Marine Corps social media Websites

It is the Marine Corps' goal to provide information and news about the Corps as well as an open forum for discussion about Marine Corps related topics.

Opinions and feedback on social media sites are welcome so long as they are presented in an objective and respectful way that allows for a continued information relationship.

While these sites provide an open forum, they are intended to maintain respect for those who participate (i.e. family-friendly). Please keep your comments clean.

Participants are asked to follow our posting guidelines below. Violation of the guidelines below may result in your post being removed.

Posting Guidelines

- *We do not under any circumstance allow graphic, obscene, explicit or racial comments or submissions nor do we allow comments that are abusive, hateful or intended to defame anyone or any organization.*

- *We do not allow solicitations or advertisements. This includes promotion or endorsement of any financial, commercial or non-governmental agency. Similarly, we do not allow attempts to defame or defraud any financial, commercial or non-governmental agency.*

- *We do not allow comments that suggest or encourage illegal activity.*

- *The appearance of external links on the site does not constitute official endorsement on behalf of the U.S. Marine Corps or Department of Defense.*

- *Participate at your own risk, taking personal responsibility for your comments, your username and any information provided.*

Make sure you understand, abide by, and monitor your site for compliance with the items listed above. It is a great way to ensure a solid standard of conduct for you and your users. Keep in mind that your users and fans won't be taking a break for the weekend. Weekend activity on Facebook is sometimes busier than during weekdays, so monitor your wall every day, even after hours on weekends and holidays.

Aside from removing posts or users who violate the rules, by keeping an eye on your wall, comments, or feedback gives you a good gauge for what your online community wants to hear about.

IT'S ABOUT THE COMMUNITY

The temptation is to send out command messages and organizational information, but it's also good to keep the page entertaining enough for people to want to follow it. Don't fall into the trap of talking at your audience. This type of communication is a conversation, not a speech.

Ask your audience for feedback and suggestions; then act on that feedback. Being social accomplishes little if your audience is not interested in what's being said. Listening to your audience can mean the difference between maintaining a successful social media presence or an irrelevant one. Take the time to respond to questions; your community will value the interaction.

 Tell people that you're out there. Attach links to your social media sites at the bottom of your press releases, in the signature block of your official emails, on your business cards, and so on. Good, old-fashioned content promotion helps spread the word about what you have to offer – and helps your community grow.

A static social media presence is ineffective. Static pages are boring and visitors to the page lose interest quickly. People won't continue to visit a rarely updated page.

Keep in mind, a large social media following doesn't happen overnight, so relax and execute your social media strategy. The better you are at providing good information and engaging your audience, the faster your following will grow.

 Connections: When someone expresses an interest in your online presence, then take the next step to have a relationship where they can be part of the conversation, they are counted as a connection. Some examples of typical social networking connections are:

Subscribers – those who sign up for your channel on YouTube
Fans – people who opt to join your community on Facebook
Followers – community of users who decide to keep track of your presence on Twitter

 Likes: When "Liking" a page on Facebook you decide to connect to that page. The benefit from liking a page allows you to have news provided from the page into your Facebook News Feed – it also allows your friends on Facebook to see that you are a fan of that page or site. On the other hand, when you click the (insert the "Like" button icon graphic here) button on a piece of content, you are that specific post, comment or topics as something you are interested in. You can "like" content without leaving a comment.

 Retweet: Information on Twitter that people find interesting generates buzz. One of the ways Twitter users share content they find useful is by resending Tweets others have posted. Re-sending a Tweets is called Retweet. This process also increases other's awareness of different communities, interests and popular trends online or in the news. Being retweeted or reciprocating other fellow Twitter user's Tweets is one of the most important ways to achieve value on Twitter.

MAINTAINING OPERATIONS SECURITY

Social media is a quickly evolving means of distributing information. Exploiting communications is a relatively inexpensive and largely effective way for our enemy to take advantage of any chance they have to do harm, wreak havoc, infiltrate systems, and so on. Because of this, it is vital that you understand what "critical information" is and how it can lead our adversaries on a path to their target. You, your fellow Marines, civilian Marines, and family members must understand the risks involved with sharing personally identifiable information, unit locations, deployment dates, or equipment specifications and capabilities.

Just sharing what you might consider to be trivial information on Facebook, Twitter, discussion threads, or blogs can be pieced together by America's enemies who scour social outlets. Keep in mind, sharing seemingly harmless information online can be dangerous to loved ones and your fellow Marines — and may even get them killed.

Our adversaries - Al Qaeda, domestic terrorists, and criminals for instance - have made it clear they are looking at our content. It is everyone's responsibility to understand, share, and communicate the risks associated with the improper use of online communications or social media outlets.

OPERATIONS SECURITY POLICY

In order to abide by the rules, you have to understand what and why they were written. In this case, the best way to stay safe and know how to protect operations security is to review the Marine Corps Operations Security Program.

For Marine Corps online content, paragraph 6 of Marine Corps Order 3070.2 (the Marine Corps Operations Security Program), provides guidance regarding unclassified, publicly available websites. The Order also defines, in great detail, what the Operations Security (OPSEC) process is and outlines a great collection of what constitutes critical information.

Through the information you distribute online, you can pave the quickest way for the bad guys to do their job. To set up some basic online protection, use the following checklist to get a handle on OPSEC.

The Social Side of OPSEC

Connect: www.facebook.com/NavalOPSEC

Stay Informed: twitter.com/#!/navalOPSEC

Get Trained: cdsetrain.dtic.mil/opsec, and www.iad.gov/ioss

Make a Plan – Army OPSEC Planner's Course: www.1stiocmd.army.mil/Home/iotraining

CHECKLIST FOR OFFICIAL UNCLASSIFIED, PUBLICLY AVAILABLE WEBSITES:

☐ Designate members of your unit to be responsible for posting content to your official unclassified, publicly available websites include your YouTube, Flickr and Blog sites. Make certain all of those assigned received OPSEC training.

☐ Your command has someone assigned as the OPSEC Officer. Ensure the OPSEC Officer reviews your command's Web site to ensure no critical information is published through the information, graphics, or photographs you post.

☐ Make sure all content for your site is approved by your commander or your release authority (Public Affairs Officer, Unit Information Officer, etc). This includes making sure all content is posted in accordance with Public Affairs guidance and the OPSEC program.

☐ Monitor your Facebook wall and comments posted to your YouTube, Flickr and Blog presences. Make sure external social media users are not posting sensitive information on your official presence. Remove all posts that contain sensitive or critical information or break the published rules for posting on your platform.

☐ Screen official unclassified, publicly available websites and make sure to remove family member information from online biographies.

☐ Ensure the only type of contact information listed is in the form of organizational charts, directories, or general telephone numbers for commonly requested resources, services and contacts — without individual's names shown. DO NOT POST DUTY ROSTERS OR DETAILED ORGANIZATIONAL CHARTS WITH NAMES, EMAILS, PERSONAL PHONE NUMBERS, ETC. The only names, phone numbers, or personalized, official e-mail addresses that can be shown are for command or unit public affairs personnel and those designated by the commander as command spokespersons.

☐ All biographies published on publicly accessible websites must be screened to make sure they don't contain any date of birth, current residential location, or any information about family members.

☐ Produce training materials and conduct regular social media OPSEC training within your unit and other units in your organization.

☐ Provide social media OPSEC training to the families of your Marines. It's important to keep them just as informed and up-to-date as the Marines in your unit.

☐ Be vigilant. Continuously review your social media and websites for OPSEC indicators or violations.

USING SOCIAL MEDIA FOR CRISIS COMMUNICATIONS

Communicating during a crisis is one of the most important things Public Affairs Marines can do to ensure public awareness and to be able to coordinate the proper resources to help with the crisis. Social media channels are an excellent capability due to their speed, reach, and direct access to all the audiences involved. Your social channels and those used by others can help distribute relevant command information to key audiences and the media while also providing a means for dialogue among the affected and interested parties. Public Affairs and Command designated personnel are the de facto lead when it comes to establishing valid crisis communication efforts. Facilitating this flow of information through social channels will help avoid erroneous, misleading or misguided content.

The time to set up the communication network, however, is not during the crisis or time of need. Plan ahead and be consistent during the crisis. Some suggestions are provided below to keep you on track: be the trusted source.

The best course of action is to leverage already existing online communication channels and social networks. It is important to send the most current, official Marine Corps updates to key audiences before a crisis hits so people know where to find you online, and trust the information they receive.

Monitor content posted by users

Regularly monitor social media sites so that you understand what information the audience or community is asking for. Answer their questions as often and as best as possible, with timely responses to ensure the audience knows they are being heard and that the Corps is working to ensure they are kept in the loop during the crisis. You should also use search engines and other monitoring tools to track discussion on the topic. Keeping yourself and your community up to date goes a long way in ensuring you can rapidly respond where and when needed the most.

Post cleared information as it comes in

When a crisis hits, there's no need to wait for a formal press release. When you have solid information that the audience needs to know, post it. Playing it too cautious and waiting for everything to play out could damage your unit's credibility.

Stay mobile

Keep social media content up to date by using mobile devices. A crisis can occur at any time, so be prepared. Coordinate with your information technology personnel to ensure you are able to access social media sites through your (issued) mobile device. You should also have a commercially available back-up prepared, such as a midi or other wireless access device. Keep your social media account access information on hand. Also ensure you have all the cords, connectors, and power solutions you'll need to operate from remote or on-scene locations.

CRISIS COMMUNICATIONS CONTINUED...

Share information
Share critical information with a network of trusted social media sites, such as the Marine Corps' official Facebook page (http//www.facebook.com/Marines) and other Marine Corps command, government, and official nongovernmental sites, like the American Red Cross. The social media community is large and it's possible to reach a lot of people through an extended network in the social media space. Promote social media presences.

Make sure to promote your social media presences on all your outgoing press releases, e-mail signatures, links on your Command and unit Web pages, and in conversations with reporters. Your social media presence isn't helpful if people don't know about it. Make sure the public knows that your social media presences are a good and trustworthy resource for information.

Encourage people on the scene to send info
Let people on the scene know they can help. They can do so by using their personal accounts to communicate the command information or feed you information to post on official command sites. No matter how the information is submitted, the command site should always promote this timely content, when appropriate.

Analyze results
Once the crisis is over, analyze what happened. Evaluate metrics and track user feedback. It's important to evaluate how your social media capabilities perform during a crisis so adjustments can be made for the future.

What to do
OPSEC breach, spill or compromise: If you think operations security is in danger or at risk, call your OPSEC program manager, local Security Manager or Command Operations Center. Any military installation security management office should be able to direct your inquiry, in the case of serious security issues or concerns.

Crisis Situation:
If the potential crisis is a local issue, contact the local authorities. For military concerns, contact the nearest operations center or public affairs office. There's also the option to leverage social media to make notification as well – through the local unit Facebook page, Twitter or Official Marine Corps Facebook page.

Public Affairs Directory: www.marines.mil/publicaffairs

Marines Official Facebook page: www.facebook.com/Marines

Social Jargon

What is...

Crowdsourcing: The practice whereby an organization motivates a variety of freelancers, paid or unpaid, to work on a specific task or problem. Closer to home, crowdsourcing has been used to identify counter-measures for enemy weapons, locate defective batches of ammunition, or even by search giant Google to help solve complex updates for a portion of its search algorithm.

Metadata: Information that supports or describes a particular item or topic. This information (data) can include titles, descriptions, tags, and captions that describe a media item such as a document, file, video, photo, or blog post. For example, metadata on a document might be the title, subject, and author whereas descriptive metadata on a computer file can include file size, the date it was created, and file type.

Hash tag: The # symbol plus a string of text, used to mark keywords or topics in a Tweet. Twitter users created the tag option as a way to categorize messages. For example, people often use a hashtag like #MilitaryMonday to aggregate, organize and discover relevant posts that pay tribute to our troops each week on Twitter. Clicking on a hashtagged word in any message shows you all other Tweets in that category. Try it out on Twitter using the tag #Marines

Podcast: A digital file (usually audio, but sometimes video) made available for download to a portable device or personal computer for playback. This can also represent a topic or syndicated show that comprises several episodes. A podcast uses a "feed" that lets you subscribe. When a new audio clip is published online you are notified, or your device that is set up to subscribe to the feed is updated. The Marine Corps maintains video and audio news, and content podcasts -- available free for download on iTunes.

RSS feed: RSS (Really Simple Syndication), sometimes called web feeds, is a standardized method to deliver online content. Feeds are offered from a variety of sources such as blog entries, news stories, headlines, or images enabling readers to stay current with favorite or required updates, without having to browse or directly visit a Web site. There are many feeds available for those interested in the Marine Corps, ranging from news and video to MARADMIN messages and policy directives, magazine articles, and blog posts. To subscribe to a Marine Corps RSS feed, visit http://www.marines.mil/feeds.

Search Engine Optimization (SEO): The process of arranging your website to give it the best chance of appearing near the top of search engine rankings. As an Internet marketing strategy, SEO considers how search engines work and what people search for.

Tweet up: An organized or impromptu gathering of people who use Twitter. Users often include a hashtag, such as #tweetup or #sftweetup, when publicizing a local tweetup event. NASA, for example, uses periodic Tweetups to provide their followers an opportunity to go behind-the-scenes at NASA facilities and events, and speak with scientists, engineers, astronauts and managers. Their Tweetups range from two hours to two days in length and include a "meet and greet" session for participants to mingle with other interested Twitter users and the people behind NASA's Twitter feeds.

Web analytics: The measurement, collection, analysis and reporting of Internet data for the purpose of understanding who your visitors are and optimizing your website.

SOCIAL MEDIA AND FAMILIES

Social media is an important tool that can keep families and Marines connected. Family Readiness Offices currently offer a wide variety of information for families. Ultimately, social media is helping to keep families connected; this is vitally important to unit well being.

WHAT CAN FAMILIES POST?

• Pride and support for service, units, specialties, and service members

• Generalizations about service or duty

• General status of the location of a unit ("operating in southern Afghanistan" as opposed to "operating in the village of Hajano Kali in Arghandab district in southern Afghanistan")

• Links to published articles about the unit or service member

• Information in the public domain so long as it doesn't violate privacy of others or doesn't compromise operations security.

 Pay close attention to what is being talked about and avoid restating what looks like it might be unsafe for families or Marines. If someone appears to be talking about topics that shouldn't be shared, a courteous post reminding them of operations security might serve as a helpful reminder to them and for others to remember safety considerations.

KEEPING OUR MARINES – AND OURSELVES SAFE

There are terrific opportunities in online communities to connect with Marines who are deployed, communicate about Marines who are fighting for our Nation, and express pride in loved ones who are serving in the Corps. The downside is that there are now more opportunities than ever to unknowingly put ourselves and our Marines in harm's way through what might seem to be innocent discussions on Facebook or other online social outlets.

Facebook brings command information to the family through a medium that they already use - which is why it works so well. On that particular platform, you can see your grandma's updates, your sister-in-law's kid's pictures, and get an update on how your son is doing while deployed with the Marine Expeditionary Unit, all in one place. The trouble is, others can gain access to this same content – all in one place too. Those "others" aren't looking to join in the discussion, though, they are looking for ways to compromise Marines and detract or destroy military success. One way they do this is by harming those that the Marines rely on – their families. They may also use the information you post to locate and injure Marines. Other nefarious uses include stealing your identity, using the information to infiltrate government networks, or other forms of illegal or dangerous actions.

Facebook is not considered a family readiness tool for Family Readiness Officers or unit personnel. The platform is a good way to communicate and hold open discussions, but it is far too open a forum to share and discuss specific details about where Marines are located, who they are, who their family members are, when and where a unit will be pulling into port, when Marines are returning from deployment, etc. This platform is however, one you can leverage for outreach to the community of family and friends interested in your unit.

OPERATIONS SECURITY FOR MARINES OR FAMILIES – ISN'T THIS A MILITARY-ONLY THING?

The Marine Corps could not do our jobs without the support and concern of family members and the military community. You may not know it, but you also play a crucial role in ensuring your loved ones' safety just by what you know of the military's day-to-day operations. You can protect your loved ones by protecting the information that you know. This is known in the military as, "Operations Security," or OPSEC.

What is OPSEC?

OPSEC is keeping potential adversaries from discovering critical Department Of Defense information. As the name suggests, it protects US operations - planned, in progress, and those completed. Success depends on secrecy and surprise, so the military can accomplish the mission more quickly and with less risk. Enemies of freedom want this information, and they are not just after the military member to get it. They want you, the family member.

Unofficial Websites

The posting of pictures and information that is pertinent to your loved one's military unit to personal or family websites has the potential to jeopardize their safety and that of the entire unit. Coordinate with your unit's Family Readiness Officer to have pictures screened so they can be posted to the "Official" unit Family Readiness website. This will ensure that you contribute to OPSEC and keep the force safe.

What Information is Sensitive?

The following list provides examples of sensitive or critical information that may help you in defining how to communicate safely. There are many more examples, but the list below gives a good baseline of what to avoid posting:

• Detailed information about the mission of assigned units.

• Details concerning locations and times of unit deployments.

• Personnel transactions that occur in large numbers (e.g., pay information, power of attorney, wills, or deployment information).

• References to trends in unit morale or personnel problems.

• Details concerning security procedures.

Talking about or sharing minor or casual details of unit or Marine information may seem insignificant. However, to a trained adversary, this information contains small pieces of a puzzle that highlight what U.S. forces are doing and planning. Remember, the elements of security and surprise are vital to the protection of Department of Defense personnel, and to the accomplishment of U.S. goals.

Where and how you discuss sensitive information is just as important as with whom you discuss it. An adversary's agents tasked with collecting information will frequently visit some of the same stores, clubs, recreational areas, or places of worship that you do. They can also easily collect data from cordless and cellular phones and even baby monitors using inexpensive receivers available from local electronics stores.

If anyone, especially a foreign national, persistently seeks information from you, notify your military sponsor immediately.

WHAT YOU CAN DO TO PROTECT OPERATIONS SECURITY

There are many countries, organizations, and individuals that would like to harm Americans and degrade U.S. influence in the world. It is possible for spouses and family members of U.S. military personnel to be targeted by these entities for intelligence collection. This is true in the United States, and especially true overseas. To stay safe from wrongdoers, keep in mind some of the following tips:

Be Alert
Foreign Governments and organizations can collect significant amounts of useful information by using spies. A foreign agent may use a variety of approaches to befriend someone and get sensitive information. This sensitive information can be critical to the success of a terrorist or spy, and consequently deadly to Americans.

Be Careful
There may be times when Marines cannot talk about the specifics of their jobs. It is very important to conceal and protect certain information such as flight schedules, ship movements, temporary duty locations and installation activities, just to name a few. Something as simple as a phone discussion concerning where a Marine is going on temporary duty or deploying to can be very useful to adversaries. Do not post details about troop movement, missions, logistics, numbers, locations, or homecoming dates whether or not your Marine is deployed. Also, avoid posting specific details about your Marine's job or occupational specialty.

Protect Critical Information
Even though some information you discuss may not be secret, it may be what the Department of Defense calls "critical information." Critical information deals with specific facts about military intentions, capabilities, operations, or activities. If an adversary knows this detailed information, U.S. mission accomplishment and personnel safety can be jeopardized. Information must be protected to ensure an adversary doesn't gain a significant advantage. By being a member of the military family, you will often know some critical information. Do not discuss these details outside of your immediate family and especially not over the telephone.

Protect Privacy
Posting personal information about Marines or recruits should be avoided. This includes but not limited to identifying information such as last names, email addresses, phone numbers (office, cell, or personal), birthdates and addresses. Always use discretion when posting any personal information. Please respect the privacy of your Marine. Posting detailed personal information about other Marine family members should be avoided as well.

Photos are important
There is a review and release process associated with all official military photographs. Even what might seem to be simple photos can disclose troop locations, equipment, tactical unit details, numbers of personnel, and much more. As a result, if you receive an image or locate a photograph of Marines involved in any military operation or exercise, you should not post the photograph unless it has been released by the Marine Corps or Department of Defense. You should also never share photographs of Marines in a deployed, operational location. A better way to connect others to Marine Corps photos is to link to images on official Marine Corps or DoD web sites.

Protecting privacy extends to everyone. Social venues provide an easy forum to intentionally or accidentally violate privacy, including: intrusion (physical or electronic intrusion into one's private quarters), public disclosure of embarrassing facts (the dissemination of truthful private information which a reasonable person would find objectionable), casting someone in false light (the publication of facts which place a person in a false light, even though the facts themselves may not be defamatory) and appropriation (the unauthorized use of a person's name or likeness to obtain some benefits). Aside from violating others, you could be breaking the law. Be mindful and report violations to your Marine's chain of command.

WHAT YOU CAN DO CONTINUED...

Taking Action

What should you do if you become aware that information is being posted online which could compromise unit operational security:

- Notify your sponsor, Family Readiness Office, or the unit operations security manager immediately.

- Contact the site administrator to notify them of the issue and ask that the post or comments be removed.

- Post reminders to the community about the importance or OPSEC and point out the dangers associated with sharing critical or sensitive information.

- Remember: If you aren't comfortable placing the same information on a sign in your front yard, don't put it in an email or share online. This is not intended to limit your free speech, the purpose is to protect lives and safety.

- Marines, families and the Marine Corps depends on you to maintain OPSEC. If you're uncertain as to what you can or can't share online or in email conversations, please contact your Family Readiness Office.

Tips for making safer social media posts:

Example post:	Change to:
My Marine is in Afghanistan at Camp Xyz.	My Marine is deployed to Afghanistan.
My Marine will be leaving Kuwait and heading to Afghanistan in three days.	My Marine deployed this week.
My Marine is coming back at 1130 am on the 15th of July.	My Marine will be home this summer.
My family is back in Jacksonville, NC.	I'm from the East Coast.

Are you telling everyone where you are?

Location-Based Services are used more and more by social networking sites that find the geographical location of a mobile device, tablet, or other communication method through GPS or Wi-Fi to provide offers or services based on this information. This might be helpful to alert you to a great sale or deal from a nearby vendor. It might also be an interesting challenge or habit to check in to a location on services like Foursquare or Facebook Places. There are dangers associated with this capability, however. For a detailed description on how to check some of these settings, please see the previous inset regarding Facebook Places.

There are no current, immediate Marine Corps-related benefits to Marines or family members by using location-based social media.

GETTING PERSONAL UPDATES ABOUT INJURED MARINES

Notifying families that their Marine has been injured or has died is not the job of social media. Making sure that families have priority from Casualty Assistance Calls Officers and Marine Corps staff is extremely important and vital to the Corps. This type of information should NEVER be shared through social media channels.

Social media channels cannot assume to have complete knowledge about which family members have and have not yet been informed about official Marine Corps notices. Even if you believe that sharing the information you have will be timely and helpful, remember: you may be casually sending notice to families that weren't even aware anything negative has taken place. And, once the information is posted, there is no bringing it back and it will spread extremely fast – to others, to strangers, and to the media.

Please, let the professionals that the Marine Corps has assigned handle delivery of official notices. This allows everyone to get the best possible assistance and ensures fair and rapid care for those whom our Marines have identified as those to be first informed. Don't make this decision for the Marine by sharing their personal details online.

EVEN MORE FAMILY RESOURCES

MILITARY PERSONNEL SERVICES
Full-spectrum of military services for Marines and their families

go.usa.gov/bvw

UNIT, PERSONAL & FAMILY READINESS PROGRAM
Commanding Officers at all levels are required to maintain this program for their unit, including a full-time Family Readiness Officer (FRO) who provides a link between the Commander, Marines, families, resources & support organizations both on and off base.

www.usmc-mccs.org/upfrp/

MARINE CORPS FAMILY TEAM BUILDING
Supports the Family Readiness Program Readiness and Deployment Support Training, Family Readiness Program Training, Lifestyle Insights, Networking, Knowledge, and Skills (L.I.N.K.S.) Training, and Life Skills Training and Education. Resources are available on all Marine Corps installations.

www.usmc-mccs.org/mcftb/

FAMILY ADVOCACY PROGRAM
Provides counseling to Marines and their families dealing with issues ranging from anger management to stress management, parenting, and couples communication. Support services also help with challenges Marine families face such as frequent deployments, ongoing relocations, and separation from family and friends.

www.usmc-mccs.org/famadv/

EMARINE – A SAFER WAY FOR FAMILIES TO CONNECT ONLINE

The eMarine website, part of the Commandant of the Marine Corps initiative to improve organizational communication, is the Corps' safe, secure, portal for dissemination of official family readiness information. The system is available only to Marines and their Family Members.

Similar to Facebook, Twitter, YouTube, and Flickr the eMarine portal provides its members a tool to access documents, view photos and videos, participate in forums, and gain important information about their Marine's Unit from anywhere in the world.

Each eMarine site offers an online community that can be customized for each Marine Corps Unit and is maintained by the Unit Commander and Family Readiness Officer. System content is assessed by command personnel who are obligated to ensure they look out for the Marine Corps' and your best interests when it comes Operations Security – adding even more safety to your communications.

HOW TO GET STARTED

For Marines – Keep your family informed about your unit by registering yourself in eMarine. After you're signed up, you can sponsor up to five family members. Anyone you sponsor is automatically approved for your Unit's eMarine site. You can also manage your sponsor list online, anytime.

Your process is simple:
• Register for your unit's eMarine site.
• Log in to eMarine at http://www.emarine.org
• Select Getting Started > Invite Family Members.
• Enter the names and email addresses for your family members and choose your Unit to join them. They will be added to your family member list and an invitation email will be sent for them to register.
• Once they register, they're automatically approved for your Unit's site.

For Family Members – Ask your Marine to send you an invitation to eMarine. Then follow the instructions to subscribe.

• Or, you can visit http://www.emarine.org
• Select the "Find a Unit Site" button.
• Click "Sponsor Search."
• Enter your Marine's first name, last name and date of birth then click "search."
• Choose your Marine's unit and follow the instructions to subscribe as a Family Member.

Anyone a Marine lists an as a family member in the Family Readiness module of Marine On Line (MOL) can subscribe to eMarine. In this case, no invitation is necessary, the family member will be able to request access as long as they know their Marine's first name, last name and date of birth. Unit Family Readiness Officers will validate the request against data saved in Marine On Line before granting access.

BLOGGING

TO BLOG OR NOT TO BLOG?

There are many reasons to deliver your message or content through a blog: a need to provide commentary, news, personal accounts or editorial perspectives, or more informal (and perhaps brief) topics of discussion.

One of the most significant benefits of offering a blog is providing a place to build a community where your readers can interact, comment and discuss topics that are relevant and important to your organization, unit or Command. If you are not prepared or not interested in accepting comments, you may want to reconsider if a blog is really the most appropriate tool for your communications objective.

Before you commit, keep in mind there are considerable resources involved in managing a blog. A successful blog needs dedicated resources, time, and staff to moderate comments and make it an effective communication tool. It also requires content and posting commitment. Irregular and infrequent blogging eventually fails.

Considerations BEFORE you decide to establish a blog:
• You must consistently write and publish content often enough to keep an audience informed and interested. Do not use press releases as a substitute for actually writing a post that will engage your audience. Aim to average at least one posting per week.

• Must have the available staff or time to review blog posts for typos, grammatical errors, and content clearance. Staff must manage the blog, including writing and reviewing blog entries, moderating all comments in a timely fashion, monitor blog metrics, and promote the blog posts and topics.

• Be prepared to moderate and review comments to:
  • prevent spammers from posting harmful links to sites that might contain malware.
  • filter for personal attacks and offensive content.

• Have the ability or aptitude to manage the blog design and technical details ranging from layout to plug-ins, and various media tools.

SAMPLE TYPES OF BLOG POSTS

• *Explanatory* – Tell a story as an engaging way of explaining a complex process or concept.

• *Interview* – Interview an expert, leader, or newsmaker. Interview posts are a way to share the expertise or opinion from a credible source that may not have time to write for your blog.
Example: http://marinesmagazine.dodlive.mil/2010/06/28/sgt-majbradley-a-kasal/

• *Profile* – Focus on a particular case study, organization or interesting personality and the characteristics that have lead to success.
Example: http://marinesmagazine.dodlive.mil/2011/11/21/war-pig-homes-cramming-comfort-into-life-on-the-road/

• *Informational* – Share articles, Websites, postings, etc. that relate to your topic by summarizing, interpreting, or linking to other content on the Web.
Example: http://marines.dodlive.mil/2011/11/16/marines-strengthen-aussie-alliance/

- *Contrasting Perspectives* – Outline both sides of a perspective, project, service or approach.
  Example: http://marines.dodlive.mil/2011/05/07/becoming-a-marine-mom/

- *Success Stories* – Tell a story of success or paint a picture of what could be. These posts can be inspirational and motivational. Your audience can share ideas, resources, or stories on similar experiences.

- *Event Blog*- Information about a progressing current event over the course of several weeks or even several hours.

- *Solicit Ideas*- Ask your audience for input on a future project or feedback on a project as it progresses.
  Example: http://marines.dodlive.mil/2010/12/28/where-real-marines-are-made/

SETTING UP A MARINE CORPS BLOG

If your unit, organization or command decides to establish a blog, you may be eligible to for a blog site on the Department of Defense blog platform (DoDLive) through the Defense Media Activity.

To get started, download and complete the blog request form and Memorandum of Agreement and email them to Marines@dma.mil.

The Marine Corps social media staff will review the agreement and verify your eligibility.

Once the review is complete, your agreement will be forwarded to the Public Web office for site creation and follow-on instructions (i.e. setting up your administrator account and providing guidance on design and theme options for your blog).

Download the documents from: http://marines.dodlive.mil/2011/11/29/setting-up-a-marine-corps-blog/

BLOGGING TIPS

- Write simply, concisely, and conversationally.

- Avoid acronyms, slang and jargon, unless you provide definitions.

- Limit the length of your post (typically less than 600 words.)

- Post titles should follow guidelines similar to those for headlines.

- Use categories, tags, and archives to organize your content.

- Include images in your posts (one lead image at a minimum.)

- Links within the blog are encouraged, but if linking to sites external to the Department of Defense, an external link disclaimer must be provided on the blog site or within the footer of the post.

- Avoid overwhelming the reader with facts and figures. Keep it simple and link to more details.

- Engage your readers and be responsive to their comments.

- Be committed to reading every comment received, even if you do not post a response.

15 Tips to Stay Safe and Out of Trouble Online

1. Post appropriate content.
- You are personally responsible for your actions.
- Ensure any Marine Corps content you post is accurate and appropriate.
- Remember: you lose control over content once it's posted.
- Always use your best judgment and keep in mind how the content of posts will reflect upon yourself, your command, and the Marine Corps – now and in the future!

2. Don't break the law.
- Adhere to Federal law, as well as Department of Defense, Department of Navy, and Marine Corps regulations and policies.
- Don't use any words, logos or other marks in your posts if it will infringe upon the trademark, service mark, certification mark, or other intellectual property rights of the owners.
- If you violate Federal law, regulations or policies, you are subject to disciplinary action under the Uniform Code of Military Justice (UCMJ)

3. Understand the guidelines when making unofficial posts about the Corps.
- If appropriate, identify yourself as a Marine or your affiliation with the Marine Corps, to include your rank, billet, military occupational specialty or occupational series, and status (active, reserve, civilian, contractor).
- If you decide not to identify your affiliation with the Corps, you should not disguise, impersonate, or otherwise misrepresent your identity.
- You can use Department of the Navy and Marine Corps symbols in unofficial posts so long as the symbols are used in a manner that does not bring discredit upon the Services, does not result in personal financial gain, or does not give the impression of official or implied endorsement.

4. If you wouldn't say it to your grandma, don't post it.
Don't say/post anything that could be perceived as:
- Defamatory
- Libelous
- Obscene
- Abusive
- Threatening
- Racially or ethnically hateful
- Otherwise offensive or illegal

Quick Reference Definitions:
Defamation: an intentional false communication that injures another's reputation or good name.

Libel: written/pictorial defamation (this is used if a wide audience for the defamation is possible such as: things posted on the internet)

Slander: spoken/gestured defamation.

5. Avoid spillage!
- Do not post any information that is:
- Classified (Confidential, Secret, Top Secret)
- Controlled Unclassified Information (CUI)
- Sensitive but Unclassified (SBU), For Official Use Only (FOUO), Law Enforcement Sensitive (LES), Sensitive Homeland Security Information, Security Sensitive Information (SSI), Critical Infrastructure Information (CII), etc.)
- In violation of operations security (OPSEC), such as tactics, troop movements, force size, weapon system details, and so on.
- When in doubt, contact your unit operations officer, security manager, intelligence officer, foreign disclosure officer, or public affairs officer for guidance.

6. Guard your personal information.
- Do not provide sensitive, family-related information within your profile.
- Keep your plans, schedules, and location information to yourself.
- Protect your coworkers, friends, and family members. Don't post information that would infringe upon their privacy, proprietary, or personal rights. This means: don't post their personal contact information such as email address, home address, phone numbers, social security number, or physical location.
- Tell friends to be careful when posting photos and information about you and your family. Talk to family and friends about operations security and what can and cannot be posted.
- Videos can go viral quickly; make sure they don't give away sensitive information. When using social media, avoid mentioning rank, unit locations, deployment dates, names, or equipment specifications and capabilities.
- Geotagging is a feature that reveals your location to other people within your network. Consider turning off the GPS function of your smartphone. If you're involved in an official Exercise, Operation, or deployed – turn off your mobile device GPS functions.

Don't share your:
- Social Security number
- Home address
- Birthday
- Birth place
- Driver's license number
- Other personally identifying information

- By piecing together information provided on different websites or from different responses, criminals and adversaries can use the information to, among other things, steal your passwords and identity, impersonate you, stalk you, harm you, or harm your family and your fellow Marines.
- Check all photos you intend to post for indicators in the background or reflective surfaces that may expose unwanted details.
- Double check that you want the information you are about to post to be forever available to anyone at anytime.

7. Don't share information that is not approved for public release.
- Not memos, not e-mails, not meeting notes, not message traffic, not white papers, not public affairs guidance, not pre-decisional materials, not investigatory information, not proprietary information... JUST DON'T DO IT!

8. Talk about what you know best.
- Only discuss Marine Corps issues related to your professional expertise, personal experiences, or personal knowledge.

9. Correct misinformation politely.
- Professionally and respectfully correct errors and misrepresentations made by others about the Marine Corps
- Not sure if you have accurate information to correct an error? Refer to your chain of command or public affairs office for guidance

10. Don't get political.
- If you do want to provide your political opinion, do so within Department of Defense guidelines:
- You can express your political views on public issues or political candidates online, but not as part of an organized communication campaign.
- If your communication identifies you as a member of the Department of Defense or Marine Corps you should clearly state the opinions are yours.
- You cannot solicit votes for or against a party, candidate, or cause.
- You cannot participate in any interview or discussion as an advocate for or against a party, candidate, or cause.
- Commissioned officers must avoid contemptuous words against the President, Vice President, Secretary of Defense, Deputy Secretary of Defense, Secretary of the Navy, or Governor and Legislature of any state in which he or she is located, or performing duty in — THIS IS FEDERAL LAW.
- Don't express or imply Marine Corps endorsement of any opinions, products, or causes.

11. Look out for bad guys.
- Do not click links or open attachments unless the source can be trusted!
- Cyber criminals pretend to be people they are not in order to deceive you into performing actions that launch cyber attacks, download viruses, and install malware and spyware onto government or personal computers.
- Look for "HTTPS" on the web site address and the "lock" icon on the Web page that indicate active security before logging in or entering sensitive data (especially when using Wi-Fi hotspots).

12. Don't fire and forget – review all your account and privacy settings.
- "Friends" and "followers" are considered relationships that can affect your security clearance, so make sure you only make connections with people you know well.
- Sort "friends" into groups and networks, and set access permissions accordingly. Add "untrusted" people to the group with the lowest permissions and accesses.
- Verify, through other channels, that a "friend" request was actually from your friend.
- Beware of "apps" or "plug-ins" which are often written by unknown third parties who might use them to access your data and friends.
- Applications (e.g. Farmville on Facebook) may share your personal information with other users on Facebook AND external to Facebook. Check the settings of EACH application you use before "allowing access."
- Make sure only your family and friends (people you know WELL) can see your photos, full name, and other information.
- Assume that all the information you share will be made public (meaning, someone can find it on Google!).
- Don't accept default account privacy settings. Carefully look for and set all your privacy and security options – in all your online accounts (not just Facebook).

13. Use strong passwords.
- Whenever possible, use at least 14 characters or more.
- The greater the variety of characters in your password: the better.
- Use the entire keyboard, not just the letters and characters you use or see most often.
- Have a different password for every login.
- When creating a password avoid:
- Dictionary words in any language. Words spelled backwards, common misspellings, and abbreviations.
- Sequences or repeated characters. Personal information.
- Source: Microsoft Online Safety (http://www.microsoft.com/protect/fraud/passwords/create.aspx)

14. Look out for intruders.
- Notice any changes to your account that you didn't make? Change your password immediately.
- Think about how someone may have received access to your site and make appropriate changes to avoid that in the future.
- Check your accounts daily for possible use or changes by unauthorized users.

15. Use anti-virus and anti-spyware.
- Use anti-virus and anti-spyware software on your personal computer and keep them up to date!
- Department of Navy and Marine Corps personnel can download free anti-virus software from Navy Information Assurance at https://infosec.navy.mil/av/index.jsp
- There is also free software available online*:
- AVG Anti-virus: http://free.avg.com/
- AvastAnti-Virus: http://www.avast.com/
- Ad Aware Anti-Spyware: www.lavasoft.com/products/ad_aware_free.php
- Microsoft Security Essentials: http://www.microsoft.com/security_essentials/

* No endorsement is intended, there are plenty of other free and paid for anti-virus and anti-spyware software available online.

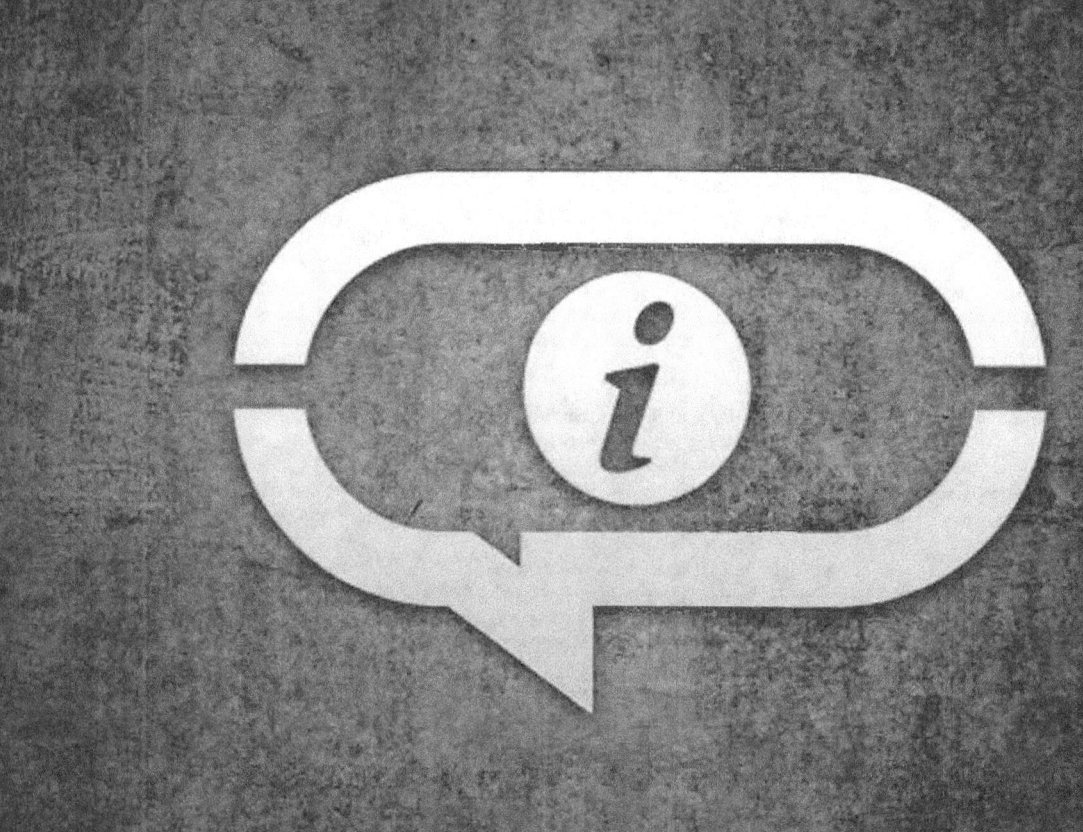

FREQUENTLY ASKED QUESTIONS

Q: How do I get content on the Marine Corps main social media sites?
A: The Marine Corps' social media team is always looking for content. You can email stories, photos or links to unit videos to Marines@afn.dma.mil and we will work to feature them on our sites.

Q: What if my unit doesn't have money or enough people to manage a social media presence?
A: Although it may only take one person to manage a Facebook page or a Twitter account, these duties can rapidly consume all of their time. Focus only on the basic social presences you can adequately dedicate resources to, and once you're committed, ensure the personnel you have assigned have the time to accomplish the mission. Consider combining forces to share social media duties with units or Commands throughout your chain of command. Establish a social media "battle rhythm" or daily/weekly schedule to ensure assigned personnel have a roadmap to follow. And outline clearly defined lateral limits to what can and can't be posted and community actions that will and won't be allowed (see "Setting Up Ground Rules" p 22).

Q: Who can manage my unit's Facebook page?
A: "Social Media Manager" is not a military occupation specialty or standard Marine Corps duty assignment so it is often viewed as an additional duty. Often times, public affairs specialists take the role of social media managers since much of the content loaded to social media sites is news and command information. The basic foundation for social media management is outlined in the Directive Type Message 09-026 (link provided in the References section).

Q: What happens if someone is impersonating me or someone in my unit?
A: Report the impersonation to the social media organization by clicking on the report button or emailing the organization directly. If the organization is unresponsive and the impersonation becomes a threat to reputation or personal safety contact the Marine Corps' social media team at the Defense Media Activity and we will assist in getting the page or profile removed.

Q: Can I delete comments on my unit's Facebook wall?
A: Every registered social media presence in the Marine Corps is required to have a posting policy in place. This posting policy should indicate what can and cannot be posted to a Facebook wall. If users violate these terms on your unit's wall, you are entitled to delete the comment and block the user if necessary. Keep in mind that communicating on Facebook is about facilitating the conversation, so stick to your posting policy, but don't delete comments just because they express negative opinions about your unit or have some profanity.

Q: How can I increase the number of individuals who follow my unit on Facebook and Twitter?
A: Be creative. There is no surefire way to increase followers on Facebook and Twitter. Different techniques work for different units or commands, so it's important to think outside the box. Ask your followers to participate in the conversation, respond to them directly and ask them what they expect out of your social media presence. Look at what other organizations are doing. If they launch a successful campaign on Facebook, feel free to use their example and tailor it to your unit. Social media is still evolving so there is a lot of room to be creative. Don't be afraid to experiment.

Q: A family member has posted something to one of the social media presences that violates OPSEC. What do I do now?

A: If you are an administrator of the page - remove the comment, related comments or underlying original post, as applicable. If you are not a page administrator in Facebook, engage the person and ask them to remove the post immediately. Explain that information isn't appropriate for conversation online. Since Facebook administrators should also scan the page for issues, also add a comment asking for their interaction. If the person refuses or persists, you have the option to block them or report them (using the "X" button on the comment or comment string). Lastly, seek guidance from your command public affairs or operations security personnel so that they are informed of the OPSEC concern and issue.

Q: My unit does not currently have a Facebook (Twitter, YouTube, etc.) account. How do I get started?

A: First, know that you're not alone. Fortunately most social media platforms are relatively easy to use. The best way to get started is to find someone you know who is savvy with social media to show you the ropes. You can also start your own personal social media accounts so that you can familiarize yourself with how they work. If you have any questions that you can't find answers to you can contact the Marine Corps social media team at the Defense Media Activity or your local public affairs office.

Q: I did some searching and found that my unit already has a non-official family group on Facebook (Twitter, YouTube, etc.). What should I do?

A: Many commands or units have unofficial social media presences established by Marines, family members, veterans, or fans that are excited about the unit. The Marine Corps does not have the right to remove these presences, nor would we want to, unless they portray themselves as an official presence. In the meantime, work with your command leadership to determine if you want to contact the page or simply monitor it and chime in when you have information to add. If you do contact the page's administrator(s), they may be eager to have your participation. Regardless, this should not stop you or the command from creating an official presence for your command and its families. Marine Corps official presences are listed in the Corps' social media directory: http://www.marines.mil/socialmedia.

References

References will be updated periodically online at http://www.marines.mil/socialmedia. However, the list of references that apply to the content in this handbook is listed below for your information and use.

Responsible and Effective Use of Internet-based Capabilities Directive Type Memorandum 09-026 (DTM 09-026)
http://www.dtic.mil/whs/directives/corres/pdf/DTM-09-026.pdf
(The Memorandum assigns responsibilities for responsible and effective use of Internet-based capabilities, including social networking services.)

Joint Ethics Regulation
Department of Defense 5500.7-R
http://www.dod.mil/dodgc/defense_ethics/ethics_regulation/jer1-6.doc

Political Activities by Members of the Armed Forces
Department of Defense Directive 1344.10
http://www.dtic.mil/whs/directives/corres/pdf/134410p.pdf

Handling Dissident and Protest Activities Among Members of the Armed Forces
Department of Defense Directive 1325.06
http://www.dtic.mil/whs/directives/corres/pdf/132506p.pdf

Department of the Navy Privacy Program
Secretary of Navy Instruction 5211.5E
http://doni.daps.dla.mil/Directives/05000%20General%20Management%20Security%20and%20Safety%20Services/05-200%20Management%20Program%20and%20Techniques%20Services/5211.5E.pdf

Marine Corps Information Assurance Program
Marine Corps Order 5239.2
http://www.marines.mil/news/publications/Pages/MCO 5239.2.aspx

Clearance of DoD Information for Public Release
Marine Corps Order 5230.18
http://www.Marines.mil/news/publications/Documents/MCO 5230.18.aspx
Marine Corps Operations Security Program

Marine Corps Order 3070.2
http://www.Marines.mil/news/publications/Documents/MCO 3070.2.aspx

Marine Corps Foreign Disclosure Program
Marine Corps Order 5510.20A
http://www.marines.mil/news/publications/Pages/MCO551020A.aspx

Responsible and Effective Use of Internet Based Capabilities
MARADMIN 181/10
http://www.Marines.mil/news/messages/Pages/MARADMIN181-10.aspx

Social Networking Sites Best Practices
http://www.Marines.mil/usmc/Pages/Forms/SNS Best Practices - C4IA.docx

Social Media Guidance for Unofficial Posts
MARADMIN 365/10
http://www.marines.mil/omg

Produced by the Marine Corps Production Directorate, Defense Media Activity, representing the Marine Corps Division of Public Affairs.

In conjunction with Headquarters Marine Corps Plans, Policies and Operations.

Engage the Community • Maintain Operations Security • Be Smart – Set the Example: In Life and Online
SEMPER FI